Reptile Keeper's Guides

RED-EYED TREEFROGS

AND

OTHER LEAF FROGS

R.D. Bartlett
Patricia Bartlett

BARRON'S

4-17-07

Acknowledgments

Many people have helped us in many ways with this book. Rick and Lynn Russell, Bill Love, Rob MacInnes, and Mike Stuhlman have generously shared information and photographic opportunities with us. Peter Seigfried of Escazu, Costa Rica, found the time to get us to some of the montane streams and forest lowlands where we could observe leaf frogs. Dennis Cathcart has been a great field companion.

We extend our sincere thanks to these individuals, and to the dedicated hobbyists who have developed techniques for the breeding and captive husbandry of these frogs.

All inquiries should be addressed to:
Barron's Educational Series, Inc.
250 Wireless Boulevard
Hauppauge, NY 11788
http://www.barronseduc.com

Library of Congress Catalog Card No. 99-043597

ISBN-13: 978-0-7641-1122-8
ISBN-10: 0-7641-1122-1

Library of Congress Cataloging-in-Publication Data
Bartlett, Richard D., 1938–
    Red-eyed treefrogs and other leaf frogs / by
R. D. Bartlett and Patricia Bartlett.
        p. cm. – (Reptile keeper's guides)
    Includes bibliographical references.
    ISBN 0-7641-1122-1
      1. Red-eyed treefrogs as pets. 2. Leaf frogs as pets. I. Bartlett, Patricia Pope, 1949– . II. Title.
SF459.F83 B38   2000
639.3'787–dc21   99-043597

Printed in China
9 8 7 6 5

Contents

Preface
2

Introduction
3

What Are Leaf Frogs?
5

Leaf Frogs as Pets
8

Obtaining Your Leaf Frogs
19

Caging
22

Feeding
28

Health
33

Breeding
37

Special Interest Groups
43

Glossary
44

Index
46

Preface

We have found the various leaf frogs—especially the remarkably beautiful red-eyed treefrog—to be wonderfully interesting and reasonably hardy terraria inhabitants. A few years ago, with the development of captive breeding techniques for red-eyed treefrogs, leaf frogs began enjoying a dramatic upsurge of popularity. Subsequent to that, a second coveted species, the painted-bellied monkey frog, made a very successful debut on the American pet market, and breeding techniques proved successful with it as well.

Although there are some thirty-seven treefrog species in this neotropical subfamily—the Phyllomedusinae—only six species are regularly available in the pet trade. Another two or three species may be sporadically available, but they are not yet well represented in captive breeding programs. The low numbers of species available is because of exportation restrictions from the countries of origin. Eventually, we hope, additional species will be available, captive bred, and their progeny available to the pet trade.

All types, from the inexpensive (and commonly available) types to the more unusual species, are wild creatures that merit the very best care we can give them. We hope that the information we have provided will make it a little easier to care for and understand these beautiful frogs.

Dick Bartlett
Patti Bartlett
Gainesville, Florida

Big and impressively beautiful, the giant leaf frog, *Phyllomedusa bicolor,* has proven difficult as a captive.

Introduction

Although amphibians have traditionally taken a backseat to reptiles in the interest of American enthusiasts, leaf frogs and horned frogs have done much to substantially narrow the gap. The graceful, quiet leaf frogs (and the beautifully intricate naturalistic terraria in which they flourish) appeal to many hobbyists who enjoy the nonaggressive nature of their pets.

In a one-decade time span, much has been learned about the keeping of several species of leaf frog. We once considered all of the species rather delicate, but have learned that with reasonable care many of them may live ten years or more. With the availability of the painted-bellied leaf frog, we have *relearned* the fact that not all frogs are well adapted to perpetually moist habitats.

And we continue to realize that we still have very much to learn regarding the herpetoculture of the king of the clan, the giant leaf frog, which, despite its bulk, usually defies our efforts to keep it successfully. In contrast, our efforts now produce at least reasonable results with the very small orange-legged leaf frogs.

With the exception of a single diverging member, the leaf frogs as a group are strongly arboreal. Many dwell in or near the forest canopy, descending to lower branches primarily to breed or forage. Those members of the genus *Phyllomedusa* (the monkey frogs) are the most arboreal, not even seeking groundwater to replenish their bladder supply prior to egg deposition. This becomes even more noteworthy when you consider that several of the subfamily members utilize reserves of body water by producing eggless capsules of water along with the normal eggs, the former apparently as antidesiccants for their clutches.

Phyllomedusa h. hypochondrialis is referred to as the northern orange-legged leaf frog.

Mucous- and toxin-producing glands are contained in leaf frogs' skin. The toxins of some species, the giant and the almost-as-big tarsier monkey frogs (*P. bicolor* and *P. tarsius*), are quite virulent. (Wash your hands after handling any of the leaf frogs.) In addition to mucous and toxin glands, the skin of at least four dry-adapted species of the genus *Phyllomedusa* contains lipid glands that produce antidesiccants.

Once you know whether a species is forest or xeric adapted (adapted to seasonally dry conditions), the information contained on these pages can be extrapolated to cover other taxa of leaf frogs should they become available.

As always, we suggest that you support domestic herpetoculture by purchasing captive-bred and captive-hatched leaf frogs whenever possible. In the long run, this will benefit us all.

Red eyes alone do not a red-eyed treefrog make! Note the horizontal pupils of this beautiful *Hyla uranochroa.* There are many additional morphological differences between this and *Agalychnis callidryas,* the red-eyed treefrog of the pet trade.

The painted-bellied monkey frog is a comparative newcomer to the pet trade.

What Are Leaf Frogs?

Leaf frogs are a wonderfully adapted subgroup of neotropical hylid frogs. They belong to the subfamily Phyllomedusinae, and are currently split into three genera—*Agalychnis, Pachymedusa,* and *Phyllomedusa.* (A fourth genus, *Phasmahyla,* was proposed in 1990, but has not been well accepted.) They are variously addressed as tree frogs, phyllomedusines, monkey frogs, or leaf frogs. There are, depending on the authority, between thirty-seven and forty-two species.

These frogs are all nocturnal, many breed in ephemeral ponds, and all have nonmelodious (to all but females of the species) single-syllabled calls.

As a group, leaf frogs range southward from Pacific southern Mexico into tropical South America. The genus *Pachymedusa,* which contains a single species, *P. dacnicolor,* ranges the farthest northward. *Agalychnis* (pronounced Ag-ah-lick-niss), with eight species, ranges from southern Mexico to Ecuador, and *Phyllomedusa* (twenty-eight to thirty-three species) ranges from Costa Rica southward to Argentina.

Despite the fact that the members of these three genera look quite different, all phyllomedusines share distinct similarities. Some of these are external and easily observable. For instance,

they all happen to have vertically elliptical pupils, and all deposit their egg masses on leaves above standing water. It is their use of leaves for their eggs, not their color or appearance, that gives these frogs their common name.

The leaf frogs of the genera *Agalychnis* and *Pachymedusa* tend to have large and well-developed toe pads and are adept at both leaping and walking through their elevated homes. Two members of the former genus have greatly developed toe and finger webs and are considered gliding frogs. One, *A. craspedopus,* has great flanges of skin on its lower jaw and the outer edges of the shanks.

The Mexican leaf frog, *Pachymedusa dacnicolor,* is the northernmost member of the group.

The eye color of *Agalychnis litodryas* gives rise to the common name of maroon-eyed treefrog.

The slender leaf frog is very appropriately named.

In contrast, the many members of the genus *Phyllomedusa* have very abbreviated webbing, slender limbs, and (with the exception of the primarily terrestrial toadlike leaf frog, *P. atelopoides*) tend to clamber in a methodical hand-over-hand method along their arboreal highways. Again, with the exception of *P. atelopoides*, all members of this genus tend to be green dorsally—at least when adult and during the daylight hours—and many have brightly colored legs or eyes. The basic coloring of the juveniles of several species becomes dark (purplish brown, often with green dorsal flecking or smudging) at night, and a few retain this nighttime coloration throughout their lives. *P. atelopoides* is the only species that is brown (flecked with green) throughout its life.

The most popular leaf frog is the red-eyed treefrog, although a more accurate name for it would be the red-eyed leaf frog. It is now followed in popularity by the painted-bellied (or waxy) monkey frog.

The forest-dwelling red-eyed treefrog was until rather recently the only phyllomedusine frog available to herpetoculturists. It has now been joined by its larger and immensely popular xeric-dwelling relative, the painted-bellied monkey frog, by the Mexican leaf frog, by the smaller and less colorful maroon-eyed treefrog, by two races of orange-legged leaf frogs, and by a species that just may take the industry by storm, the tiger-striped leaf frog. A seventh species, the Brobdignagian giant monkey frog, continues to be imported occasionally, but has proven difficult to keep.

Captive breeding means that red-eyed treefrogs are now almost always available. Depending on the time of year, they can be purchased as tadpoles, new metamorphs, or adults. All the other species are available only as juveniles or as adults, and they may cost more than the red-eyed juvenile or adult. Both the tiger-striped and the giant monkey frog have very limited availability.

Although they are very capable of leaping, red-eyed treefrogs are not particularly agile, and their relatives, the monkey frogs, are even less so. Both kinds often traverse their aerial highways in a hand-over-hand, foot-over-foot walk, even when in a hurry. Their opposable toes grasp leaves and limbs securely and tightly, providing these frogs with ample dexterity and sure-footedness.

To discourage the desiccating effects of dry breezes, the xeric painted-bellied monkey frog and other semiarid-adapted species secrete a waxy material from dermal lipid glands. Periodically, the frog rubs its hands and feet over its skin and methodically wipes all exposed areas of its body, spreading the antidesiccant. This dramatically lessens the loss of moisture through the normally permeable skin.

Many of the leaf frogs are protected by the countries in which they appear, but very occasionally a species of leaf frog not currently in herpetoculture may be collected from the wild and will appear on a specialty dealer's list. These were once "dead end" animals with no chance of being bred, but now, providing the creatures reach us in relatively good condition, our knowledge of their requirements allows us a far better chance at establishing new species in herpetoculture.

Agalychnis spurrelli, another of the gliding leaf frogs, is not yet represented in herpetoculture. This newly metamorphosed example found in Costa Rica looks quite unlike the adult of the species.

Currently, the red-eyed treefrog, *Agalychnis callidryas,* is more popular than all other leaf frogs combined.

Leaf Frogs as Pets

When you select your treefrogs, begin with the cage or aquarium in which the frog has been kept. If the cage isn't odor free, problems will very quickly become evident in the frogs. Leaf frogs kept in other than pristine conditions will absorb bacteria or ammonium-tainted water through their skin, and trying to stem a metabolic infection or chemical overload is rather like gluing together a cracked egg. It's certainly worth trying, but the results may not be what you want.

If you plan on breeding your leaf frogs, you'll have far better chances if you start with a half dozen or so. There are few morphological differences between the sexes, and they tend to be noticeable only during the breeding season. Males, during the breeding season, develop dark-pigmented horny excrudences or nuptial pads on their thumbs. These are used to help hold the female during mating. Males are usually considerably smaller than the females, and overall more angular. This is particularly noticeable during the mating season when females are holding eggs. Males are the only sex to have voices, and these are generally used in the evening or at night. The calls are not particularly melodious, but they have the desired effect on the females of that particular species. Vertical pupils indicate nocturnal activity patterns.

Blue-Sided Leaf Frog

The blue-sided leaf frog, *Agalychnis annae,* is a lowland and montane species that has been found widely in central Costa Rica, and probably lives in adjacent Panama as well. Sad to say, this is one of the signal species for the vanishing frog syndrome. *A. annae* has disappeared from areas of Costa Rica where it was once common.

Vertical pupils indicate the nocturnal lifestyle of the leaf frogs. Pictured is a red-eyed treefrog.

Females average about 3 inches (7.5 cm) in length and males about 2.5 inches (6.4 cm). They are found near woodland pools. The dorsum is a rich green, the sides and outer fingers and toes are a robin's-egg blue, the thighs are generally a deep purple, and the venter is white to off-white. The blue of the sides is bordered ventrally with yellow-orange, and the inner toes are similarly colored. The eye is a beautiful golden orange. The male's call is a rolled *wrr-rr-ok*.

Specimens are imported occasionally, but all have proven delicate. This species is not established in American herpetoculture.

The beautiful Central American blue-sided leaf frog, *Agalychnis annae,* is apparently a species in decline.

Red-Eyed Treefrog

The red-eyed treefrog *(Agalychnis callidryas)* is a beautiful phyllomedusine hylid found in forests from southern Mexico to extreme eastern Panama. Although it has been periodically imported in large numbers, it is only within the last eight years that successful captive breeding programs have made these frogs truly popular.

Females, the larger sex, attain about 3 inches (7.6 cm) in length, and males reach a snout-vent length (SVL) of about 2.25 inches or 5.7 cm. What red-eyes may lack in size, they make up for in coloration. The dorsum of a contented red-eye is often a shade or two on the chartreuse side of leaf green. White dorsal spots may be profuse, few, or lacking entirely. The amount of blue on the flanks can vary considerably from population to population. In the frogs most extensively marked, the blue can begin at and involve the apices of the forelimbs, the upper arm itself,

then extend back to the groin and anterior femur. The blue may range from robin's egg, through sky, to deep purplish blue. Sometimes the side shading is brown instead of blue. The white barring in the blue flanks can be even more variable. The vertical sections may be narrowly spaced, widely spaced, thick, thin, and either connected at top and/or bottom by horizontal white markings, or lacking the horizontal sections. The venter, underlimbs, and toes are suffused with a variable amount of golden yellow. The snout of the male is

Some red-eyed treefrogs are variably peppered with white flecks.

Limbs and leaves provide arboreal highways for red-eyed (and other) leaf frogs.

sloped from nostril to upper lip, whereas that of the female is convex in profile. The male's breeding call, which may be of one or two syllables, is a coarse *wrrok* or *wrrok-ock*.

Several quite consistent geographic differences can be noted, with the frogs in the northern populations being smaller and less intricately patterned than their counterparts from the south. Typically, northern red-eyes have orange (not blue) thighs and lack the uppermost light stripe that on southern populations isolates the blue bars on the side. Despite their consistency, these currently are merely considered geographic variables.

The vertical barring and blue sides of the red-eyed treefrog vary geographically in intensity.

Cold or otherwise stressed frogs can be quite dark in color.

If you do decide to try breeding this species, get all of your specimens at the same time, from a single dealer. This will more or less assure you that all specimens have originated from the same general area, are genetically compatible, and that the offspring will be characteristic red-eyes from a particular range, rather than "mutts."

Maroon-Eyed Treefrog

The maroon-eyed treefrog, *Agalychnis litodryas,* is a comparative newcomer in the American pet trade. It is a little smaller, with a 2-inch SVL, and much less colorful than its better-known red-eyed relative, but is a pretty and interesting species in its own right.

This is one of the most nondescript of the *Agalychnis*. The dorsum of this leaf frog is usually a yellowish green (a hue that might be considered a sickly shade on congeners), the sides and toes are pinkish, and the venter is white. There may be small, round, enamel-white spots on the dorsum. Although virtually nothing is known about the natural history of this species, it has the fully webbed hands and feet typical of other gliding species (flying frogs) in the genus. Females have a snout rounded in profile, whereas the snout of the male slopes downward from nostril to lip. The male's call is a single-syllabled belch.

This interesting frog was once considered among the rarest of the genus, and was long known from only a single specimen that originated in Panama's eastern Darien. The extent of its range has not yet been accu-

Gliding

Several species of leaf (and a few other) frogs are capable of making long gliding leaps. This ability is best developed in those species with extensive webbing between all (fore and rear) toes. To accomplish this parachuting, the frog launches itself from a high perch, extends its limbs, and spreads its fingers and toes widely. Its body is slightly below the plane of the digits. This position, creating an aerodynamically sound outline with a proportionately great surface area, enables the anuran to make very long, shallow-descending, gliding leaps.

rately defined, but probably includes much of Panama and northern Colombia.

The maroon-eyed treefrog is now being bred in considerable numbers by Rick and Lynn Russell of North Fort Myers, Florida. It has not proven entirely satisfactory as a captive, its long gliding leaps bringing it forcibly into contact with the screen sides of even the large 10-by-10-foot cages provided by the Russells.

The maroon-eyed treefrog is one of the neotropical gliding frogs.

Mexican leaf frogs are more apt to leap than many other members of the group.

Mexican leaf frogs have intricate gold iris flecking, easily seen even from a distance when the frog's eyes are open.

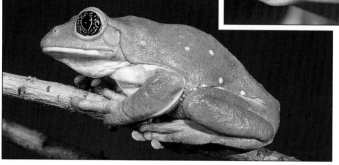

Mexican Leaf Frog

The Mexican leaf frog, *Pachymedusa dacnicolor,* is a reasonably large (females to 4 inches [10 cm]; males to 3.25 inches [8.3 cm]) leaf frog that lives farther north than any other member of the subfamily. It is a common species over much of Mexico's Pacific versant. In coloration, the adult Mexican leaf frog is a plain but pleasing green dorsally (sometimes with scattered white spots) and an off-white ventrally. The toes can have a yellowish tinge. New metamorphs and juveniles are purplish brown dorsally and have irregular green flecking. The golden yellow irises have profuse black venations. The breeding call is an unmelodious cluck.

Besides being smaller, males have a snout that angles straight down to the lip from the level of the nostrils, whereas the snout of the female is convex in profile.

In the wild, this treefrog places its egg masses on vegetation overhanging the water, on emergent and waterside grasses, on branches and on water-edge debris, and, where vegetation is absent, on the muddy banks up to several inches above the water.

The Mexican leaf frog is easily bred in captivity, having clusters of up to several hundred eggs. Albino and leucistic phases have appeared.

The giant leaf frog is occasionally collected from the wild and imported for the pet industry.

(below) This is a giant leaf frog in profile.

Giant Leaf Frog

Although it has proven delicate and difficult to keep the giant leaf frog *(Phyllomedusa bicolor),* it is occasionally seen in the American pet trade. It has an immense range, appearing in forested areas virtually across tropical South America from Colombia to Brazil.

Up to 2,000 eggs per clutch have been attributed to this species, but it seems that between 200 and 500 is more typical. Besides the viable eggs, clutches contain large numbers of the yolkless "water beads" so typically produced by the frogs of this subfamily.

This is an angular frog. Females reach 4.5 inches (11.5 cm) in length, and the males attain 4 inches (10.2 cm). It is a pretty leaf green dorsally and laterally, an off-white anterioventrally, a very pale grayish orange on the belly, and pale orange-brown on the underside of the rear limbs. The demarcation between the green lateral

coloration and the off-white ventral color is precise and defined by a thin dark stripe. The toes, hidden surfaces of the hind limbs, upper arms, and portions of the venter bear dark-edged light, rounded spots. The large eye has a silvery iris. The snout of the female is rounded in profile; that of the male is nonconvex.

Imported specimens often bear skin injuries from which they do not readily recover. The injured areas are prone to bacterial and fungal infections. These are a canopy species that suns extensively in its native habitat.

Although occasional captive specimens have survived for more than a decade, most succumb quickly. The giant leaf frog remains a problematic captive.

This species has a visible parotoid gland and produces complex and virulent toxins. Wash your hands carefully after handling it.

Orange-Legged Leaf Frogs

There are two subspecies of this pretty and quiet little frog, the southern, *Phyllomedusa hypochon-*

drialis azureum, and the northern, *P. h. hypochondrialis,* which differ marginally in the white striping of the upper lip and the extent of orange, and in lateral markings. The southern form often lacks a white stripe on the upper lip and has one or two dark longitudinal stripes in the white lateral field. Together, the two races of this frog occur over a vast area of northern, central, and southern South America east of the Andes.

This, one of the smallest of the leaf frogs, can be difficult to maintain. Males are adult at a slender 1.5 inches (3.7 cm) in length, and large females

barely attain 2 inches (5 cm). This is a strange little frog that often looks as if it is walking with its dark-flecked silvery eyes only half open. The dorsal coloration, including the tops of the legs (except for the upper arm) can vary from bright new-leaf green to a rather unpleasant olive-gray-brown. The sides are white (often with an orangish overcast), and there is a white labial stripe of variable extent. The upper arm and the hidden surfaces of the hind legs are orange with brown bars. The belly is white.

The orange-legged leaf frog is a denizen of relatively rain-impover-

The typical hand-over-hand method of movement is demonstrated in these three photos by a southern orange-legged leaf frog.

Northern orange-legged leaf frogs are persistently nocturnal.

By day, northern orange-legged leaf frogs are often clad in hues of brown.

The slender leaf frog, *Phyllomedusa lemur,* is one of the smaller members of its genus.

ished llanos, chacos, and the pampas, and does not do well in humid situations. It requires very small food insects.

Clutches contain from thirty to about eighty yolked eggs, but like many of the more arid-adapted leaf frogs, this species also produces many more nonyolked, water-containing capsules in each clutch.

Despite its delicacy, both races of *P. hypochondrialis* are being captive bred in some numbers.

Slender Leaf Frog

This plainly colored leaf frog, *Phyllomedusa lemur,* is so slender that it appears emaciated. It is found on Costa Rica's Atlantic versant and adjacent Panama. Like most phyllomedusines, the slender leaf frog is capable of considerable color change, being grayish brown dorsally with greenish spots at night and a rather bright green during the day. The groin is orange or yellow. The venter is white. Males are about 1.5 inches (3.7 cm)

in length, and females are some half inch (1.25 cm) longer. Because of year-round rains, this species has a poorly defined breeding season. Clutches can number up to thirty-five eggs, but are often only half that number. The breeding call is a single hoarse quack. This species is not established in American herpetoculture.

Note the toxin-secreting shoulder (parotoid) gland of this painted-bellied monkey frog, *Phyllomedusa sauvagei.*

Painted-Bellied Monkey Frog

Hand-over-hand, foot-over-foot, a painted-bellied monkey frog makes its way along a limb.

This beautiful frog, known scientifically as *Phyllomedusa sauvagei* and often referred to as the waxy monkey frog, has gone from a virtually unknown herpetocultural entity as late as the mid-1990s, to one of the most intensely bred leaf frogs in the late '90s. It is fairly large, quite pretty, and very hardy, a suite of characteristics difficult for American herpetoculturists to overlook. The hardiness came as somewhat of a surprise, for until its recent availability, this species had a reputation of delicacy. Perhaps, before we realized that this was a low-humidity-adapted frog, we tried to keep them too moist, a situation untenable to this species.

The painted-bellied monkey frog hails from Paraguay, Bolivia, Argentina, and adjacent Brazil. It is a heavy-bodied species. Females attain a length of a little more than 3 inches (7.6 cm) and have a rounded nose when seen in profile; males have a sloping nose and reach about 2.5 inches (6.5 cm).

This species is one of the plainer-colored leaf frogs, but its bold chest pattern of dark-edged white bars on green lends an air of interest. The belly, the lower lip, the edge of the upper eyelid, and the outer edges of the limbs are white. The dorsal coloration is a pleasing bright leaf green. The voice consists of a coarse primary note that may be followed by several softer secondary notes.

The breeding grasp of the leaf frogs (pictured are painted-bellied monkey frogs) is called amplexus.

Here we see two stages in the development of the large tarsier leaf frog, *Phyllomedusa tarsius*. The tadpole with hind legs (and front legs about to emerge) is first, followed by a newly metamorphosed example.

During his visits to Paraguay, Mike Ellard, an importer of reptiles and amphibians, reported finding adults of this frog during the dry season sitting on sparsely leafed limbs, in a brisk breeze, in the full sunshine, at temperatures near or just over 100°F. This is not the kind of scenario that we usually think of for a frog.

This species has now been bred by herpetoculturists in California and Florida. The Florida breedings were accomplished by Rick and Lynn Russell in outside wire mesh cages with dimensions of about 2 feet wide by 2 feet deep by 5 feet high. The frogs were kept indoors during the winter and put outdoors in the spring. The eggs were placed in rolled leaves of a hanging basket of pothos. More than 600 viable eggs, as well as the yolkless water-holding egg capsules, are contained in a typical clutch.

Tarsier Leaf Frog

The tarsier leaf frog, *Phyllomedusa tarsius*, looks much like a deeper green, dark-eyed (coppery red with strong black vermiculations), rough-skinned version of *P. bicolor*. The venter is brownish anteriorly, shading to a brownish orange posteriorly. The hidden surfaces of the legs are green but bear cream to orange spots. This leaf frog has immense parotoid glands and produces complex skin toxins. Females attain 4.25 inches (11.2 cm) in length; males are somewhat smaller. The tarsier leaf frog seems to be restricted in range to Colombia and Peru, but may occur farther to the east. Clutches containing more than 500 eggs have been found. This species is unknown in American herpetoculture.

Tiger-Striped Leaf Frog

Phyllomedusa tomopterna, the pretty tiger-striped leaf frog, is the new contender for popularity supremacy on the American pet frog scene. Simply put, we feel it will be a strong candidate because of the ease with which it is bred and its attractiveness. This is another species in which females attain a length of about 3 inches (7.6 cm) and males are about half an inch (1.25 cm) shorter.

This is a forest frog that breeds in newly freshened swamps, temporary pools, and even cavities in logs. Clutches contain up to seventy eggs.

The vocalization is a chucking note with little carrying power.

The dorsal color of *P. tomopterna,* including the sides of the face, the shoulders, and the dorsal surfaces of the limbs, is a bright green. The throat and chest are white, and the belly is orangish. The flanks and hidden surfaces of the limbs, upper arms, fingers, and toes are variably orange with strong purple-brown vertical barring. Each heel bears a prominent calcar (dermal spur), and the iris is silver. Males have a nonconvex snout that slopes in a straight line from the nostrils to the upper lip; the snout of the female is seen to be convex in profile.

The tiger leaf frog ranges widely through much of tropical South America.

The tiger-striped leaf frog, *Phyllomedusa tomopterna,* is another newcomer to the American pet trade. It is slender, angular, and slow-moving.

Obtaining Your Leaf Frogs

Leaf frogs can be obtained in many ways, but except for the occasional availability of red-eyed treefrogs, they are seldom available at neighborhood pet stores. The most reliable sources for most species are specialty dealers, captive breeder expos, or the breeders themselves.

Pet Stores

Pet stores—especially those with expanded reptile departments—now often carry red-eyed treefrogs of all sizes. We advocate purchases from neighborhood pet stores when possible because of the convenience and the customer's ability to discuss the leaf frogs in which they are interested. Such things as routine care are easily covered. There are times when, despite his or her efforts to provide accurate information, the pet store employee might err. In the store's defense, the employee may just be repeating information given him or her by their supplier. Remember, your local pet shop is often two or even three or four times removed from the initial dealing that placed the specimen in the pet trade.

Reptile and Amphibian Expos

Herp expos are now held in many larger cities across the United States and are becoming popular in Europe. An expo is merely a gathering of dealers and breeders all under one roof. One of the largest is the National Reptile Breeders' Expo, with more than 450 tables, which is held in Florida every August. Captive-bred leaf frogs of several species are usually available at these gatherings.

Leaf frogs, such as this red-eyed treefrog, can rest as comfortably on nearly vertical leaves as on horizontal surfaces.

In coloration, red-eyed treefrogs are among the most spectacular of the leaf frogs.

Breeders

Breeders may vary in size from hobbyists who produce only one or two clutches of leaf frogs each year, to herpetoculturists such as Bob Mailloux or Rick and Lynn Russell, who produce from hundreds to thousands of babies of several species each year. Search for breeders in the classified or pictorial ads sections in specialty reptile and amphibian magazines (see Special Interest Groups, page 43). Breeders usually offer parasite-free, well-acclimated specimens and accurate information. Most keep records of genetics, lineage, fecundity, health, or quirks of the species with which they work, and especially of the specimens in their breeding programs.

Specialty Dealers

As the popularity of amphibians and reptiles continues to grow, more specialty dealers have sprung up. These dealers often breed fair numbers of the amphibians and reptiles they offer, and deal directly with other breeders, but they may be direct importers as well. Specialty dealers usually try to acclimate and stabilize imported specimens before offering them for sale.

This is a vibrantly colored example of the red-eyed treefrog.

A red-eyed treefrog rests on a banana leaf.

Out-of-Area Purchases

Even with today's proliferation of herp expos, the expos, larger breeders, and specialty dealers are still not readily available to many small-town hobbyists. If you are a little off the beaten path, and if your local pet store cannot accommodate your wants, going to an out-of-area vendor may be the answer.

Check the Internet. Instruct your search engine to seek "leaf frogs," "red-eyed treefrog," or "monkey frog." You should learn of a variety of breeders, some of whom place excellent photos on their Web sites.

Dealers and hobbyists list their available livestock in the classified ads of the several reptile and amphibian, and pet magazines. Local breeders may advertise in the classified section of your newspaper.

Ask friends and fellow enthusiasts for recommendations about the reptile dealers they know. Ask about them at nature centers, museums, zoos, or among hobbyist groups. Herpetologists are a close-knit group. You'll be surprised by how many of us know each other.

After learning that your potential supplier has a satisfactory reputation, request a price list (often available automatically on the Web), and contact the supplier/shipper to finalize details. He or she will be happy to discuss prices and shipping costs with you.

Caging

If you merely wish to maintain a few leaf frogs in a healthful, simple manner, the caging need not be complicated. A 10-gallon tank with a damp paper towel on the bottom and containing a small water dish and a leafy potted philodendron or schleffera will suffice.

However, if you wish to breed these beautiful frogs, or have an artistic eye and enjoy naturalistic terraria, the terrarium will need to be more complex.

Basic Requirements

Leaf frogs do not prefer great amounts of moisture in their cage, being more at home with a relatively dry substrate and a small dish of clean water. No matter what type of caging you provide, the need for cleanliness in any amphibian caging facility cannot be overemphasized. All amphibians have permeable skins through which moisture is absorbed. If any bacteria or chemicals—such as ammonia or any other water-soluble compound—are present, they'll be absorbed as well. A dirty cage will most assuredly exact its toll on the lives of your leaf frogs.

Leaf frogs are nocturnal. By day, they usually sleep soundly, scrunched down, eyes tightly closed, and feet drawn beneath them. They feel most secure when they can feel concealed by branches or plant leaves. The frogs will awaken and hunt at night.

Although solid covers such as glass will certainly elevate the humidity of a terrarium and prevent the frogs' escape, they also prevent air cir-

Note the slender limbs and angular appearance of the red-eyed treefrog.

Giant leaf frogs are persistently nocturnal, very arboreal, and move slowly and methodically.

culation, an untenable situation. We urge that a top be made of screening or wire mesh, to allow full ventilation. Humidity can be controlled by misting the tank lightly; what you don't want are standing droplets of water. Misting will, of course, be more frequent in arid situations or air-conditioned rooms than in the humid southeastern United States or in foggy regions.

We suggest terraria of at least 10-gallon capacity for one or two leaf frogs. If more leaf frogs are to be maintained, increase the tank size to 29 to 75 gallons. The larger tanks lend themselves particularly well to naturalistic setups. Besides foliage plants, provide perches such as sterilized driftwood or gnarled manzanita (do not use cedar or any limbs treated with fungicides or insecticides).

In addition to misting, water can be provided in a shallow bowl. The water bowl should be scrubbed and fresh water provided every second or third day (more frequently if the water is dirtied). In moving around the tank at night, leaf frogs will smear the glass panes of their terrarium. Use water from your mister and paper towels to clean the glass.

A Mention of Tadpoles

From the day they hatch until metamorphosis, the tadpoles of leaf frogs are aquatic. They are easily cared for during most of their tadpole stage,

but as metamorphosis approaches, specialized care is necessary (also see pages 41–42).

A tadpole's aquarium should be set up and maintained in precisely the same manner as an aquarium for fish. Water quality, including the removal of chlorine and chloramine, is very important. A pH of 7.0 is suggested. Newly hatched tadpoles are weak swimmers, so filtration should not be so strong that they are carried into the mechanism.

Tadpoles feed readily on tropical fish staple flake food.

The Woodland Terrarium

Woodland or rain forest terraria will suit the needs of most leaf frogs well. The woodland terrarium provides only a shallow dish or two of water sunk nearly to the rim in the substrate for the frogs. The land area has a base of an inch or so of pea-sized river rock, over which a piece of

Red-eyed treefrog tadpoles give no indication of the beauty that develops soon after metamorphosis.

With good reason, the tiger-striped leaf frog has become a coveted species.

screening or air-conditioning filter material is laid. Placed atop this is 1 to 3 inches of clean soil—soil containing no insecticides, spectricides, fungicides, Styrofoam beads, or time-release fertilizer. The deeper the layer of soil, the easier it will be to add plants such as philodendron, syngonium, spathiphyllum, or fittonia. If it is available, a layer of verdant woodland moss may be added over the soil. For xeric-loving species such as the orange-legged monkey frog and the painted-bellied monkey frog, omit the moss and use only a small water dish.

You may also use a substrate consisting of only a few inches of orchid bark or cypress mulch into which the plants can be set while still in their pots. The substrate can be washed or discarded, as desired.

Since leaf frogs are very much utilizers of a three-dimensional habitat, we suggest that vertically oriented terraria be provided when possible. Aquaria are now built that are as high as or even higher than they are long, but normal aquaria may be positioned on end to create a vertically oriented environment. When this is done it will be necessary to secure a 3-inch-high barricade or piece of glass across the lower portion of the tank with Silastic to prevent the gravel and soil from falling out, and to provide a suitable front.

The front can be easily provided by setting your terrarium on blocks or legs an inch or two above the surface on which it is sitting. A tightly fitting framed front can then be merely slipped over the open side and held in place with typical top clips.

Outdoor Caging

Where climatic conditions allow, an outdoor cage of wood and wire can be provided. This well-ventilated construction prevents what would almost assuredly be lethal buildups of heat if glass or Plexiglas were used. Additionally, it permits the anurans to take limited amounts of unfiltered sun and, if the cage has a wire top, to be stimulated by falling rains. In Florida, the cages of humidity-adapted species such as red-eyed and maroon-eyed treefrogs are misted at least once daily. The cages of the more xeric painted-bellied and orange-legged monkey frogs may be sprayed only once weekly. When wood and wire terraria/cages larger than table-top size are built, we have found it a good idea to incorporate large casters into their design so that they may be easily moved about. In warm climates, where the leaf frogs can remain outdoors for most or all of the year, we have successfully used large "step-in" caging for keeping and breeding them. The wire used is ⅛-inch mesh hardware cloth. The small mesh of the wire prevents the escape of all but the smallest feed crickets. If left outdoors during cool weather, in-cage heaters are activated and the cages are wrapped in clear 4-ml-thick vinyl. This is stapled in place on three sides, but can be rolled up and out of the way or removed from the top and south side (door side) if desired. In such setups, many leaf frogs will bask for hours on sunny uprights of the frame or may leisurely bask on the horizontals of the door frame.

The bottom can be left bare, or a low frame can be installed that will retain a clean substrate such as a sand-soil mixture, orchid bark, or cypress mulch. Although we do use a sand-soil mixture on the bottoms of the cages, it is merely piled deeply and allowed to seek its own level (including being washed out) during storms. We also utilize hardy potted plants (cycads, ficus, and hanging baskets of pothos [*Epipremnum*]) within the cages. The hanging baskets are placed above large, shallow trays of water. These provide decoration and visual barriers and can be used for egg deposition. Most species soon feel secure enough in these setups to breed naturally, with no artificial inducements whatever.

The various leaf frogs breed readily in the Russells' outdoor, vertically oriented cages.

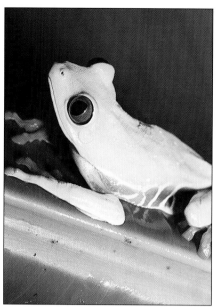

Leaf frogs, as shown by this red-eyed treefrog, are quite capable of descending a nearly vertical leaf in a head-down position.

Do not use pine oil or other phenol-based disinfectants for cleaning your frog cages or cage furniture. Likewise, do not use cedar mulch or furniture. Phenols are not tolerated well by any herps, and even the lingering odors can be fatal.

Are Supplemental Lighting and Heating Necessary?

Lighting is probably more necessary for the well-being of the terrarium plants than for the nocturnal leaf frogs. Lights will, however, provide some heat during cold weather. Rather inexpensive in-line thermostats or rheostats can be installed by electricians. Plug-in timers are readily available at hardware stores. Heating pads, heat tapes, and undertank heaters are all readily available. Do not use hot rocks for amphibians!

An ideal daytime terrarium temperature is between 75 and 85°F. Nighttime temperatures can be several degrees cooler. It is best to provide a thermal gradient (warm to cool) within any terrarium.

Greenhouses

Although they can still be expensive, greenhouses are no longer the luxury items they once were. Greenhouses of many styles, constructed from several types of materials, are readily available today—and some are even relatively affordable.

Greenhouses vary from simple, self-standing, fully constructed types available from storage-shed dealers, through myriad do-it-yourself kits, to elaborate and decorative commercial kinds that, unless you are very "handy," are best left to contractor setup. There is, perhaps, no better caging for leaf frogs than a greenhouse setup. Greenhouses are usually considered permanent structures, and a building permit may be required to legally install one.

Absolute escape-proof security is essential. Escape routes are especially possible in greenhouses made of panels of corrugated fiberglass or plastic. You must ascertain that the top and bottom of every corrugation in every panel has been sealed. Some of the more inexpensive greenhouses may have the sharp tips of screws protruding into the inside. To prevent injury to jumping frogs, each protruding

Limb dexterity allows leaf frogs great mobility in the trees.

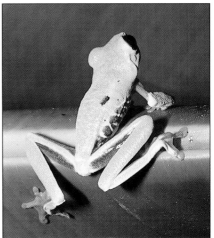

Young Mexican leaf frogs are colored very differently than the adults.

screw must be capped or tipped with a bead of silicone sealant.

Additionally, in most areas of the world, heating and cooling units must be provided, and frogs' access to these must be denied, in a safe manner. Frogs can be cooked, desiccated, or overchilled by improperly baffled temperature control units.

In all cases, double glazing should be considered as an energy-saving option, especially in regions subject to extreme cold or heat. We further suggest that the base of the unit be either flush against a concrete slab, affixed to a concrete or brick wall, or sunk a foot or more below the surface of the ground. This will preclude easy access by outside predators and escape by

the creatures with which you are working.

Greenhouses typically exemplify the adage that the grass is always greener elsewhere, and can bring a few square feet of the tropics to even the snowbelt. It is important to provide the appropriate watering, heating, and lighting systems, cage furniture, and plantings (in the case of leaf frogs, Neotropical all, philodendrons, anthuriums, selaginellas, ficus, and pepperomias can, in time, form intricate tangles). The possibility and feasibility of providing a small pond and waterfall, often much-wanted accouterments, should be well thought out at the beginning. Well-planned ponds and waterfalls can be aesthetic and feasible additions to a forest theme greenhouse that would be impossible to construct in any other setting.

When approached with imagination and forethought, the interior of even a small greenhouse can become the focal point of your home and a wonderful home for a collection of leaf frogs.

Feeding

When adult, the various leaf frogs are insectivores. In captivity, all can be acclimated to feed on commercially available insects such as mealworms, crickets, wax worms, and flies. If for any reason—such as during shipping—your leaf frog has been deprived of food or water for a lengthy period, it may need considerable prodding to start it feeding and drinking again. It will be your responsibility to offer fresh food and moisture in such secure and calming surroundings that your specimen just cannot resist the temptation. Once the frog has been rehydrated and has begun feeding again, it is likely that it will continue to do so. It may even expand its horizons to a food type quite different from that which is natural to it.

Insects

At first, finding a few crickets or houseflies or grasshoppers is easy, but when confronted with the task of finding insects in the wild week after week, you will probably decide that purchasing is much easier.

Non-noxious insects (avoid fireflies and ladybugs) fed fresh from the wild will need little if any vitamin or mineral augmentation to benefit your leaf frogs. However, this is not the case with insects held captive for long-term frog food. To provide your frogs the necessary nutrients, those insects must be fed well and continuously. A poorly fed or otherwise unhealthy insect offers little but bulk when fed to a reptile or amphibian. You may watch your frogs or toads eat feed insects every day, yet if the insects are not healthy, the amphibians may be slowly starving or developing a malady such as metabolic bone disease.

Dust crickets fed to adult frogs with a vitamin/mineral supplement (calcium and vitamin D_3) at least once weekly—and dust those fed to fast-growing metamorphs at least twice weekly.

Tailor the insect size to that of your frogs (small frogs, small insects; larger frogs, larger insects).

Before mentioning specific care for several of the more commonly used food insects, let's discuss "gut loading." Insects, be they crickets, mealworms, or other insects, must be fed an abundance of highly nutritious foods throughout their captivity, and especially immediately before being offered as food to your frogs. Foods high in calcium and beta-carotene (a vitamin D_3 precursor) should be a large part of the insect's diet. Fresh fruit and vegetables (such as carrots), fresh alfalfa and/or bean sprouts, honey, and vitamin/mineral-enhanced (chick-) laying mash are only a few of the foods that may be considered for gut-loading insects. A commercially prepared gut-loading diet is now available in many pet stores.

Field Plankton

Insects straight "from the wild" are already well fed. These insects have been able to choose their diet, and their nutritive value reflects this. Field plankton is quite probably the very best diet that you can offer your leaf frogs, but acquiring this diet can quickly become tedious. Field plankton is merely a mixture of the various insects and other arachnids that can be field collected in any given location. To gather them, you simply sweep a suitably meshed field net back and forth through tall grasses or low shrubs after first ascertaining that the area is pesticide free. After having fed naturally, on natural, native foods, these insects are probably at their pinnacle of health and will greatly benefit your leaf frogs.

Crickets

Gray crickets (*Acheta domesticus*) can form the basic diet for your leaf frogs. Other cricket species are readily collected in small numbers beneath debris in fields, meadows, and open woodlands. If available in suitable sizes, all species of crickets are ideal amphibian foods.

If you need only a few crickets, they can be purchased from local pet

or bait shops. If you use several hundred to several thousand crickets weekly, purchase them from wholesale producers that advertise in fishing or reptile magazines. You will find that the prices are quite reasonable when crickets are purchased in multiples of 1,000, and having them delivered to your house is very convenient.

Crickets must be fed a well-rounded diet if they are to benefit your leaf frogs. Feed the insects a good and varied diet of your own making (fresh carrots, potatoes, broccoli, oranges, squash, sprouts, chick-laying mash), or one of the nutritious, specifically formulated cricket foods on the market. Crickets can also be offered vitamins and minerals on their foods, not so much for their benefit as for the benefit of the amphibians to which the crickets are fed. Crickets will drown easily if they are given just a plain, shallow dish of water. Instead, place cotton balls, a sponge, or even pebbles or aquarium gravel in the water dish. These will give the crickets sufficient purchase to climb back out when they fall in.

This is a Panamanian example of a red-eyed treefrog in profile.

Keep crumpled newspapers, egg-crate inserts, or the center tubes from paper towel rolls in the crickets' cage. We prefer the paper towel tubes because they can be lifted and the requisite number of crickets shaken from inside them into the cage or a transportation jar. This makes it easy to handle the fast-moving, agile insects. A tightly covered 20-gallon long tank will temporarily house 1,000 crickets. A substrate of sawdust, soil, vermiculite, or other such medium should be present. This must be changed often to prevent excessive odor from the insects, and to help avoid die-offs.

Crickets are easily bred and adults are easily sexed. Females have three projections from the rear of their abdomen and males have two. The center projection of the female is the ovipositor—the organ she thrusts into the ground and through which the eggs are expelled. Keep the cricket cage between 76 and 86°F. Place a shallow dish of slightly moistened sand, vermiculite, or even cotton balls on the floor of the cage. The material in this dish will be the laying medium and will need to be kept very slightly moistened throughout the laying, incubation, and hatching process. Cricket eggs will hatch in eight to twenty days, the incubation time varying by cricket species and tank temperature. Nutritious food should always be available to the baby crickets. Once you get started, you'll find uses for all sizes of the crickets. Pinhead-sized crickets will form the base of a suitable diet for newly metamorphosed leaf frogs, the half-grown sizes are good for the smaller adults, and the adult crickets are the right size for the adult leaf frogs. Feed your frogs at night and provide the crickets with an easy egress from any water dish into which they might tumble.

Grasshoppers/ Locusts

Grasshoppers and locusts (*Locusta* sp. and *Shistocerca* sp. in part) are widely used as reptile and amphibian foods in European and Asian countries, and are commercially available there. In the United States, you'll have to breed them or collect them in the field with a net. However, grasshoppers are fast, and it may take some time for you to hone your netting skills. You may wish to remove the large "hopping" legs before you place these insects in with your frogs.

There are in the southern United States a few species of large, slow grasshoppers called lubbers. Many of these have a brightly colored (often black and yellow or red) nymphal stage that can be fatally toxic if eaten by your specimens. The tan and buff adults seem to be less toxic, but we suggest that they not be used as a food item.

Wax Worms

The wax worm (*Galleria* sp.) is really a caterpillar, the larval stage of the wax moth that infests neglected beehives. These are available commercially from many sources. They are frequently used as fish bait and are available from bait stores. Check the ads in any reptile and amphibian magazine for wholesale distributors. Some pet shops also carry wax worms.

If you buy wholesale quantities of wax worms, you will need to feed

them. Chick-starting mash, wheat germ, honey, and yeast mixed into a syrupy paste will serve adequately as the diet for these insects.

Giant Mealworms

Giant mealworms (*Zoophobas* sp.) are the larvae of a South American beetle. They have proven to be a great food source for many leaf frogs.

Zoophobas larvae can be kept in quantity in shallow plastic trays containing an inch or so of sawdust. They can be fed a diet of chick-starting mash, bran, leafy vegetables, and apples.

To breed these insects, place one mealworm each in a series of empty film canisters or other similar small containers (to induce pupation) that contain some sawdust, bran, or oats. Nestle the film containers together in a larger box, simply to keep them together and so they don't turn over; you don't really need lids, because the larvae won't climb out. After a few days the worms will pupate, eventually metamorphosing into fair-sized black beetles. The beetles can be placed together in a plastic tub containing a sawdust substrate and some old cracked limbs and twigs for egg laying (the female beetles deposit their eggs in the crevices in the limbs). The beetles and their larvae can be fed vegetables, fruits, oats, and bran. The mealworms will obtain all of their moisture requirements from the fresh vegetables and fruit.

Although giant mealworms seem to be more easily digested by anurans than common mealworms, neither species should be fed in excess.

Mealworms

Long a favorite of neophyte reptile and amphibian keepers, mealworms *(Tenebrio molitor)* contain a great deal of chitin and should actually be fed sparingly. They are easily kept and bred in plastic receptacles containing a 2- to 3-inch layer of bran (available at your local livestock feed store) for food and a potato or apple for their moisture requirements. It takes no other special measures to breed these insects.

Roaches

Although these can be bred, it is almost as easy to collect roaches as needed. Roaches, of one or more species, live in much of the world. The size of the roach proffered must be tailored to the size of the leaf frog being fed. A meal of several small roaches is usually better for your specimen than a meal consisting of one or two large roaches.

Termites

These are an excellent food for newly metamorphosed leaf frogs. Collect these pestiferous insects fresh as necessary. Should you decide to hold "extras" over, they may be kept in some of the slightly dampened wood in which you originally found them. Termites are most easily collected during the damp weather of spring and summer from behind the bark, or in the moldering wood of dead pine trees. Termites may be easily trapped and collected from wet corrugated cardboard "sandwiches" left near infested pine trunks.

Fruit Flies

Breeding stock of these tiny dipterids can be purchased from a biological supply house or collected from the wild. Biological supply houses will be able to supply you with flightless "vestigial-winged" fruit flies, a genetic mutation that makes handling this insect much easier. Mashed fruit and agar (a seaweed derivative) are good foods. These are an excellent food for newly metamorphosed leaf frogs.

Houseflies

These may be collected as needed (weather allowing) in commercial fly traps or may be bred. Tightly covered, widemouthed gallon jars are ideal for this latter purpose (be sure to punch air holes through the lid). The larvae (maggots) will thrive in overripe fruit and vegetables or other such medium. Both larvae and adult flies can be fed to your specimens. The simplest method of introducing the adult flies to the cage is to place the entire opened jar inside the cage. By using this method, fewer will escape. The maggots can be removed by hand or with forceps and placed in a shallow dish in the amphibian tank. Fly larvae are also commercially available.

The stance of this walking painted-bellied monkey frog is typical of all members of the group.

Health

Selecting Your Leaf Frog

Although leaf frogs are typically more slender than many other frogs, there is in this slenderness an inherent strength and resilience. Never purchase a leaf frog that moves spastically, appears bloated, or is too weak to jump or walk steadily.

Leaf frogs are creatures to be appreciated visually, not handled. Their skin is delicate, requires a degree of moisture, and may be easily injured. If it does become necessary to move a specimen, do so with extreme care and with clean, wet hands. Small specimens can be shepherded into a suitable fine-meshed net or a disposable plastic cup. Larger specimens can be grasped firmly, but gently, in the hand, fingers wrapped around the waist. Tadpoles must be kept in chlorine/chloramine-free water and are best caught in an aquarium fishnet of suitable size.

The color and behavior of your leaf frog may help you diagnose the cause of what could be a potential problem. Frogs too cold or too wet are often very dark in ground color. Frogs too hot may be very light in color. Frogs inactive over long periods of

Some northern orange-legged leaf frogs may assume pastel hues.

time may be too cold or too dry. Learn the body language of your leaf frog and treat it accordingly.

Proper Hygiene

These are the two words and the one act that, if stringently followed, will do more to protect your leaf frogs from illness than any other effort.

If kept clean and at temperatures (75–85°F) suitable for the species involved, frogs in general are remarkably resistant to diseases and illnesses. Wash your hands carefully before, between, and after *all* handling.

Dehydration

New imports may arrive dehyrated. Occasionally one of your own frogs may escape and evade detection for some time. Since these little creatures need continuous replenishment of their body moisture to sustain life, dehydration can quickly lead to death. Leaf frogs are more resistant to dehydration than many other species, but still require some moisture.

Remove any dust or dirt clinging to the frog by holding it under some gently flowing room-temperature water. Place the frog in a closed container (to increase atmospheric humidity) with a shallow covering of water on the bottom. Check it every three or four hours, and change the water if it becomes soiled. If not too dehydrated, the frog may absorb the needed moisture and perk up. Place it in its regular cage when it does, usually after twenty-four hours.

Insecticides

Both aerial and topical insecticides will kill amphibians. Do not spray near their cage, and never handle your frogs if you have mosquito repellent or other topical insecticide on your hands.

Gas Bubble Disease

Gas bubble disease may occur when water is supersaturated with gases. The tadpoles will bloat and their undersides may bear a red rash. Tadpoles may be unable to submerge, and the disease can be fatal. There is no direct cure. Aged water will have released extra gases to the atmosphere, but if fresh water must be used, something as simple as roiling with an air-stone or a drip-system for an hour or so before you use it will help remedy the situation. Whenever possible, let the water sit for a couple of hours before you use it.

Kidney Disease

Kidney disease or malfunction can cause an irreversible bloating in frogs. The causes are likely manifold, but sitting in unclean water and eating diets high in fat seem to be major contributors. It is therefore more often seen in aquatic frogs than in leaf frogs and more often in frogs fed a preponderance of pinkies than in those frogs fed insects and worms. Quite recently, a form of blindness caused by lipid buildups on the corneas has been seen in some frogs that have been fed a diet of predominantly pinky mice. No remedy has been found, but a suitably low-fat (natural) diet would seem to be a preventative.

Healthy red-eyed treefrogs are bright-eyed and alert.

This Panama specimen of red-eyed treefrog has very dark eyes.

Rick Russell photographed this baby red-eyed treefrog peering from the shelter of a *Paphiopedilum* bloom.

Spastic Imbalance

Spastic imbalance, as demonstrated by convulsions, tetanic leg extensions, and lack of coordination, may be attributed to a multitude of causes, but among these unclean water seems to figure prominently. Cleanliness of a leaf frog's quarters is absolutely essential!

Shedding

Skin shedding occurs periodically, and the frog will eat its own shed. This behavior is normal.

Redleg

Redleg is a bacterial disease that can rapidly prove fatal. Since it can be communicable, isolation of any infected frogs is mandatory. The pathogen *Aeromonas* is often but not always implicated. Cleanliness and a suitable temperature regime will nearly assure that this disease is never encountered; conversely, fouled water and land areas, and inordinate chill will rather assure its onset. Tetracycline hydrochloride baths are an often-used home remedy, but pathogen sensitivity tests followed by treatments done by a qualified reptile veterinarian are better.

Cuts and Lesions

Cuts, scrapes, bruises, and lesions may be of mechanical or bacterial origin. For the former two, a mild antibiotic salve or weak methyline blue (50 percent of the strength suggested for fish) may hasten healing, and removing the object causing the injury will prevent recurrence. Another remedy is a solution of sulfathiozole (one capsule of this aquarium medication to a liter of water) misted onto the afflicted areas daily. Nervous frogs may, when startled, leap repeatedly into the sides of their terrarium (seldom the case with leaf frogs) and cause repeated snout bruising. Covering the clear side of the tank with sheets of paper will help lessen this tendency. Veterinary assessment is suggested for the lesions. The cause needs to be identified and eliminated.

Intestinal Impaction

Intestinal impaction may occur if an overzealous frog ingests gravel or sand while feeding. Small amounts of sand or an isolated small piece of gravel will usually be passed by the frogs without intervention. Larger impactions may require surgical removal.

Fungus Infections

Fungus infections (usually a *Saprolegnia* sp.) may infect the wounds or scrapes of tadpoles. They can be treated topically by removing the specimen from the water and daubing Mercurochrome (2 percent), hydrogen peroxide (full strength), or malachite green (2 percent) on the area with a cotton pad and returning the tadpole to the water. Methyline blue as recommended for aquarium fish may also be used in the water. Repeat daily until the lesions are gone.

Metabolic Bone Disease

Metabolic bone disease (MBD) may occur in amphibians that do not get enough calcium/D_3 in their diet. This is especially true in rapidly growing young specimens. The prevention is simple—feed calcium/D_3-enhanced diets. The cure is less simple. Once sufficiently advanced to be observable, the insidious progression of this deficiency may not be reversible. Consult a veterinarian about injectable calcium treatments.

Endoparasites

Leaf frogs may host a number of endoparasites. These include, among others, round-, tape-, and pinworms. Because of the virulence of the treatments and the small size of most amphibians, talk to a veterinarian for both diagnosis and treatment. In many cases, skin daubs may be preferable to internal purges.

Veterinarians

We strongly urge that you find a qualified reptile/amphibian veterinarian before you actually need one. It is not usually easy to do so, and it may be too late if your frog is ailing.

Breeding

Leaf frogs are tropical and subtropical anurans with a rather specialized reproductive biology. In the wild, female leaf frogs deposit their egg clusters on leaves or lianas hanging over standing water. If on a leaf, the female will fold the leaf's edges over the clutch, thus allowing less desiccation while providing greater camouflage. A similar egg deposition site must be provided for captives.

The arboreal egg masses are contained within a gelatinous outer coating. The tensile strength of the gelatin deteriorates over the incubation time. When the tadpoles hatch, they are able to wiggle free and can drop into the water. There they develop in what we will call a typical manner. If the egg mass has been placed where the tadpoles miss the water when they drop, and if they cannot reach the water after a very few energetic wriggles, the larvae succumb.

In the wild, gravid female leaf frogs are often courted by several males. In captivity, greater breeding success may be had if several male leaf frogs are maintained with a single female. The jostling and grappling of the males seems to induce greater fer-tility. In larger settings such as a greenhouse, communal breeding involving a dozen or so males to several females can be very productive.

Leaf frogs breed seasonally, usually following a period of winter semi-dormancy or dry season rest. During this period the frogs continue to be occasionally active and to feed; they do not brumate, but only reduce their activity. Hormonal changes occur with the increasing hours of daylight (lengthening photoperiod) and at the advent of the rainy season. In the wild, of course, the changes occur

Painted-bellied monkey frogs are occasionally blue in color. The bulges behind the eyes are parotoid glands.

As with these painted-bellied monkey frogs, breeding is usually a communal affair.

An amplexing pair of northern orange-legged leaf frogs is forming a leaf funnel for their eggmass.

naturally. In captivity, depending on your setup, the changes may need to be simulated.

Males of the various leaf frogs often arrive at the breeding puddles before the females. Their short, coarse "chucks" (often single-syllabled, sometimes two or more notes), often voiced from arboreal positions, both advertise to other males and draw the females of the species to the sites. If the pond is among trees, males often make their way to it along branches. If in the open, the site must be accessed terrestrially. Females often arrive several hours after the males. If a female finds a particular male attractive—or if she's too slow to move away when approached—she will be grasped or amplexed by the male. Male leaf frogs utilize a breeding embrace just behind the female's front legs. This is termed *axillary amplexus*.

Following the seasonal cycles is relatively simple for most owners of leaf frogs—often involving little more than letting the natural rhythms of the seasons set the pace. At all latitudes, save for the actual equator, winter brings about a reduction of photoperiod, a relative drop in temperatures, and a concurrent drop in humidity. To keep your leaf frogs on their natural cycle, simply follow winter's pace for photoperiod, and provide a relative drop of temperature and humidity.

To create spring and summer, increase the hours of illumination, the temperature, and the humidity. Using a recirculating pump and a spray head, provide summer's night rains for a couple of hours a night.

When you follow the calendar of the seasons, you will have the recommended ninety-day regimen of winter conditions that seems to prepare the frogs for the stimulation of the breeding season. Winter's nighttime lows should be about 62–66°F and daytime highs in the low 70s. Winter's humidity should average about 50 percent. The night lows of summer should be in the low to mid-70s and highs in the low to mid-80s.

During their winter's activity reduction, your leaf frogs will quite probably require less food of smaller size than in summer. Once the summer's elevated photoperiod, temperature, and humidity are begun, the misting should prompt ovulation and spermatogenesis within a week or two.

Their vocalizations may be discordant, but because male choruses are stimulating to female leaf frogs, we suggest that you tape the calls of your males and use the tapes to stimulate chorusing and, ideally, breeding, at other times.

Depending upon the species, clutches contain from 20 to more than 600 eggs. Captive females may use plant leaves overhanging their pond or, if no plant is available, will often choose a spot several inches above the water on the aquarium glass for a deposition site. This has proven precarious, because condensation on the glass can cause the eggs to dislodge and fall into the water. Eggs that do so die. It is better to gently remove the eggs from the glass (this can be done soon after the eggs are laid by slowly sliding a dampened single-edge razor blade beneath the

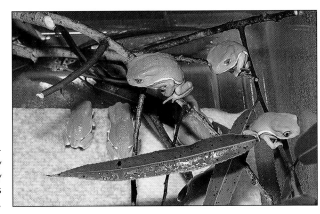

These baby painted-bellied monkey frogs were bred by herpetoculturists Rick and Lynn Russell.

cluster, keeping the blade tightly against the glass). Place the eggs on a plant's leaf, and place the leaf in its own tank, a few inches above a bowl of suitably pure water. Keep the air surrounding the repositioned egg cluster humid by partially covering the tank with a sheet of plastic wrap or a pane of glass.

Even when the eggs are placed in an ideal spot, the space constraints inherent in captivity mean that active adult leaf frogs are apt to knock a cluster into the water. We suggest moving these also, clipping the entire leaf on which they have been laid from the plant. Again, position these in their own tank, a few inches above a bowl of suitably pure water. An alternate approach is to have the frogs in a separate tank for breeding and move the *frogs* out after egg deposition. Do keep in mind that the tiny newly hatching tadpoles will need to be able either to drop directly into the water or to reach the water within a few flips of the body after hatching. Tadpoles denied access to the water after hatching will die.

More than a single clutch of eggs (often three or four) may be deposited in a single night, or on subsequent nights, by the females of some leaf frogs. The female of the genera *Agalychnis* and *Pachymedusa* carries the quiescent male (sometimes more than one) on her back from site to site (often for more than one night), and may sit for lengthy periods in the water between depositions to replenish the water in her bladder.

Certainly, adequate water is necessary to assure the proper consistency of the jellylike outer egg casing. However, female leaf frogs of the genus *Phyllomedusa* do not sit in the water prior to egg deposition. The glutinous "jelly" is clear; the eggs themselves are greenish.

The water quality for the tadpoles must be maintained at all times. Aged water is best, but fresh, dechlorinated water will often suffice. Gentle aeration will help release the saturated gases. Filtration or daily partial water changes will help assure continued suitability. The water temperature must be appropriate for the species involved. Normal room temperature (74–78° F) is usually satisfactory for the incubation of the eggs and tadpoles of temperate or high altitude

A baby tiger-striped leaf frog balances on Lynn Russell's fingertip.

Leaf frog tadpoles are always aquatic (red-eyed treefrog, bottom; tarsier leaf frog, top).

species, whereas a temperature of 80–85°F is better for the eggs and tadpoles of tropical frogs.

As the hours progress, the eggs will change from tiny gelatinous-coated circular dots to tiny, comma-shaped, embryonic tadpoles. With passing days the gelatin discolors. Unfertilized eggs will turn white and may "fuzz up" with fungus. You can manually remove these infertile eggs or leave them in place until the fertilized eggs hatch. Once the tadpoles wriggle free of the encasing gel, you'll need to begin feeding them as they use up their reserve yolk. Raising tadpoles is achievable if food levels and water quality are maintained and space factors are considered.

Tadpoles

The time taken for the development of the eggs and growth and metamorphosis of the tadpoles will be largely dependent on temperature (78–85°F seems ideal). Hatching can

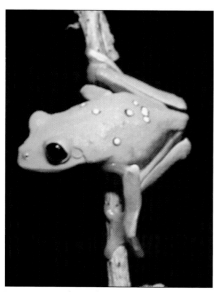

Maroon-eyed treefrogs are subtly colored, but attractive. Many have a profusion of white spots on their backs.

downward. The tadpoles of some *Phyllomedusa* have curious upturned mouths that easily draw floating matter from the surface film. The time period from hatching to metamorphosis takes nearly two months.

The newly metamorphosed leaf froglets have round (rather than vertically elliptical) pupils and often lack the intricate patterns and diagnostic colors of the adults. For example, newly metamorphosed red-eyed treefrogs have round pupils and yellow, not red, irides (irises). It may take nearly three weeks for the elliptical pupils and red irides to develop.

Within a few days after becoming froglets, the metamorphs will have developed an almost insatiable appetite. Because of this rapid growth rate, the metamorphs are especially prone to MBD (metabolic bone disease) at this stage of their lives. Feed them heavily and frequently, and dust food items with a good quality D_3/calcium mixture once a week.

Be certain you have a ready and steady supply of tiny feed insects available before you breed these (or any other) frogs. The newly metamorphosed babies are little more than eating machines, and they die very quickly without food.

occur in as few as five or as many as eleven days. The tadpole stage can last from forty to sixty days. Tadpoles will eat large quantities of good-quality fish food, including koi, trout, and catfish chows. The tadpoles of *Agalychnis* and *Pachymedusa* position themselves in midwater in a characteristic head up with the tip of the tail 45 degrees

Special Interest Groups

Herpetological Societies

Reptile and amphibian interest groups exist in the form of clubs, monthly magazines, and professional societies, in addition to the herp expos and other commercial functions mentioned elsewhere.

Herpetological societies (or clubs) exist in major cities in North America, Europe, and other areas of the world. Most have monthly meetings; some publish newsletters; many host or sponsor field trips, picnics, or indulge in various other interactive functions. Among the members are enthusiasts of varying expertise. Information about these clubs can often be learned by querying pet shop employees, high school science teachers, university biology department professors, or curators or employees of herpetology departments at local museums and zoos. All such clubs welcome inquiries and new members.

Two of the professional herpetological societies are

Society for the Study of Amphibians and Reptiles (SSAR)
Department of Zoology
Miami University
Oxford, OH 45056

Herpetologist's League
c/o Texas National Heritage Program
Texas Parks and Wildlife Department
4200 Smith School Road
Austin, TX 78744

The SSAR publishes two quarterly journals: *Herpetological Review* contains husbandry, range extensions, news on ongoing field studies, and so on, whereas the *Journal of Herpetology* contains articles oriented more toward academic herpetology.

Hobbyist magazines that publish articles on all aspects of herpetology and herpetoculture (including lizards) are

Reptiles
P.O. Box 6050
Mission Viejo, CA 92690

Reptile and Amphibian Hobbyist
Third and Union Aves.
Neptune City, NJ 07753

Glossary

Aestivation: A period of warm weather inactivity; often triggered by excessive heat or drought.

Allopatric: Not occurring together but often adjacent.

Ambient temperature: The temperature of the surrounding environment.

Amplexus: The breeding grasp.

Anterior: Toward the front.

Anus: The external opening of the cloaca; the vent.

Aposematic: Brilliantly contrasting colors that supposedly warn predators of toxicity or other danger.

Arboreal: Tree-dwelling.

Brumation: The reptilian and amphibian equivalent of mammalian hibernation.

Caudal: Pertaining to the tail (with tadpoles).

Cloaca: The common chamber into which digestive, urinary, and reproductive systems empty and that itself opens exteriorly through the vent or anus.

Con-: As used here, a prefix to several words (generic, specific) indicating "the same." (*Congeneric* refers to species in the same genus; *conspecific* indicates the same species.)

Crepuscular: Active at dusk or dawn.

Cryptic: As used here, having an outline, color, or both, that blends with a chosen and specific background.

Deposition: As used here, the laying of the eggs.

Deposition site: The spot chosen by the female to lay her eggs.

Dichromatic: Two-color phases of the same species, often sex-linked.

Dimorphic: A difference in form, build, or coloration involving the same species; often sex-linked.

Diurnal: Active in the daytime.

Dorsal: Pertaining to the back; upper surface.

Dorsolateral: Pertaining to the upper sides.

Dorsolateral ridge: A glandular longitudinal ridge on the upper sides of some frogs.

Dorsum: The upper surface.

Femur: The part of the leg between hip and knee.

Form: An identifiable species or subspecies.

Genus: A taxonomic classification of a group of species having similar characteristics. The genus falls between the next higher designation of "family" and the next lower designation of "species." *Genera* is the plural of *genus*. The generic name is always capitalized when written.

Gular: Pertaining to the throat.

Hybrid: Offspring resulting from the breeding of two species.

Hydrate: To restore body moisture by drinking or absorption.

Hydration chamber: An enclosed high-humidity chamber used to help desiccated frogs rehydrate.

Hylid: A treefrog.

Intergrade: Offspring resulting from the breeding of two subspecies.

Juvenile: A young or immature specimen.

Labial: Pertaining to the lips.

Lateral: Pertaining to the side.

Melanism: A profusion of black pigment.

Metamorph: Baby anurans, recently transformed from the tadpole stage.

Metamorphosis: The transformation from one stage of life to another.

Middorsal: Pertaining to the middle of the back.

Midventral: Pertaining to the center of the belly or abdomen.

Nocturnal: Active at night.

Nuptial excrescence: The roughened thumb, wrist, and forearm grasping pads of reproductively active male anurans.

Oviparous: Reproducing by means of eggs that hatch after laying.

Phalanges: The bones of the toes.

Poikilothermic: A species with no internal body temperature regulation. The old term was *cold-blooded.*

Polliwog: Tadpole

Posterior: Toward the rear.

Race: A subspecies.

Species: A group of similar creatures that produce viable young when breeding. The taxonomic designation that falls beneath "genus" and above "subspecies."

Subdigital: Beneath the toes.

Subspecies: The subdivision of a species. A race that may differ slightly in color, size, scalation, or other criteria.

Sympatric: Occurring together.

Taxonomy: The science of classification of plants and animals.

Terrestrial: Land-dwelling.

Thermoregulate: To regulate (body) temperature by choosing a warmer or cooler environment.

Tympanum: The external eardrum.

Vent: The external opening of the cloaca; the anus.

Venter: The underside of a creature; the belly.

Ventral: Pertaining to the undersurface or belly.

Ventrolateral: Pertaining to the sides of the venter (belly).

Note: Other scientific definitions are contained in the following two volumes:

Peters, James A. *Dictionary of Herpetology.* New York: Hafner Publishing Co., 1964.

Wareham, David C. *The Reptile and Amphibian Keeper's Dictionary.* London: Blandford, 1993.

Index

Agalychnis 5
  annae 8–9
  callidryas 7, 9–10
  craspedopus 5
  littodryas 10–11

Breeding 37–42

Caging 22–28
  aquarium (for tadpoles) 23
  basic 22–23
  greenhouse 26–27
  outside 25–26
  terraria 23–24
    woodland 23–24

Feeding 28–32
  insects 28–32
Frog
  leaf
    blue-sided, 8–9
    giant 2, 12–13
    gliding 11
    Mexican 11–12
    obtaining 19–21
    orange-legged
      northern 13–15
      southern 13–15
    slender 15
    tarsier 17
    tiger-striped 18
    what is a 5–7
  monkey
    giant (see giant leaf frog)
    painted-bellied 2, 16–17

Glossary 44–45

Health 33–36
  cuts and lesions 36
  dehydration 34
  diseases 34, 36
  endoparasites 36
  hygiene 33
  impactions, intestinal 36
  insecticides, danger of 34
  redleg 35
  selecting your leaf
    frog 33
  shedding 35
  veterinarians 36
Heating 26

Lighting 26

Pachymedusa 5
  dacnicolor 11–12
Phasmahyla 5
Phyllomedusa 5
  atelopoides 6
  bicolor 12–13
  hypochondrialis 13–15
  hypochondrialis
    azureum 13–15
  lemur 15
  sauvagei 3, 16–17
  tarsius 17
  tomopterna 18

Special interest groups 43

Tadpoles 23
Treefrog
  maroon-eyed 10–11
  red-eyed 9–10